The Mission of Jesus

Scripture text from
The Contemporary English Version

Master Books

Light!

Mary presents the infant Jesus to Simeon who had come to the Jerusalem Temple, guided by the Spirit. The use of clear colors and contrasting white lends the power of clarity to the composition. The flexible forms of the characters reinforce the delicacy and charm of the scene. These characteristics make Sebastian Bourdon one of the painters of the seventeenth century who best represents French pictorial talent.

Sebastian Bourdon
(1616-1671),
The Presentation at the Temple

© Lauros-Giraudon, Louvre Museum, Paris (France)

Someone Was Expected

The Nativity, Church of Saint-Vulfran (France)

When Jesus was born in Judea 2000 years ago, the Romans had control of the land that was inhabited mostly by Jews. The Roman rulers and the Jewish religious leaders were happy with the situation. But many of the commoners were dissatisfied. They hoped for something better — more political freedom and a more visible sense of God's presence. Israel's early prophets* had preached that one day someone would come and change things. He would be sent by God as the Anointed One, the expected Messiah, the Christ of God. The Temple of Jerusalem was the center of the Jewish religion. Young and old alike went there to pray.

According to the Law of Moses, every first-born son was to be presented there forty days after his birth. In obedience to the Law, Mary and Joseph brought Jesus to the Temple.

What Did Jesus Come To Do?

Luke the Evangelist** most likely wrote his Gospel some seventy years after the birth of Jesus. Luke writes to the people who had not seen Jesus with their own eyes and who didn't understand fully who he really was. Luke wants to tell them three things:

1. Jesus was the Messiah (or the Christ), the one they had waited for so long.
2. To understand this truth, we need the help of God's Spirit.
3. Jesus came not only for his own people (Jews), but for all people on earth.

The Evangelist Saint Luke, stained glass of the Lampaul-Guimilau Church (France)

* Prophets
People who speak in God's name as a messenger are called prophets. The best known of Israel's early prophets are Isaiah, Jeremiah, Ezekiel, and Amos.

** Evangelist
Each of the four evangelists or gospel writers had his own way of writing about the life and teachings of Jesus. The four evangelists are Matthew, Mark, Luke, and John.

3

Simeon and Anna

Luke 2.25-38 (excerpts)

At this time a man named Simeon was living in Jerusalem. Simeon was a good man. He loved God and was waiting for God to save the people of Israel. God's Spirit came to him and told him that he would not die until he had seen Christ the Lord.

When Mary and Joseph brought Jesus to the temple to do what the Law of Moses says should be done for a new baby, the Spirit told Simeon to go into the temple. Simeon took the baby in his arms and praised God,

"Lord, I am your servant,
    and now I can die in peace,…
With my own eyes I have seen
    what you have done
    to save your people….
Your mighty power is a light
    for all nations,
and it will bring honor
    to your people Israel.

Jesus' parents were surprised at what Simeon had said….

The prophet Anna was also there in the temple…. Night and day she served God in the temple by praying and often going without eating.

At that time Anna came in and praised God. She spoke about the child Jesus to everyone who hoped for Jerusalem to be free.

God's Spirit

Luke often brings God's Spirit into his Gospel. God's Spirit helps us to understand who Jesus is, what he did and what he asks of us today.

All Nations

The message of Jesus is not simply addressed to Israel (his people). It is a light for all people on earth. This light is with us today.

Anna

Together with Simeon, the evangelist presents the prophet Anna. He wants to show that women as well as men helped reveal the mission of Jesus.

The Salvation of the World

Messiah

Jesus is the Messiah, the one sent by God to redeem mankind, in fulfillment of Israel's early prophets. Jesus came to pay the penalty for sin by dying on the cross, and in so doing, helps us conquer the fear and reality of death. God's word tells us that by believing that Jesus is God's son, and that God raised him from the dead, we inherit eternal life.

Light

Sometimes thick, dark clouds block the light of the sun. In the dark, we seem to be lost and find it hard to move ahead. We are confused about what to believe. We don't know which road to take. We wonder how to shake off despair and find happiness. We don't know where to look for God. Jesus lights the path so that it can be seen again. He is the light of God and the light of the world. He makes things bright and clear and keeps us from getting lost.

Nations

The light of Jesus is not limited to only a few people. It lights the entire world and every person of every nation on earth. His light is not denied to anyone. Jesus comes on behalf of God to offer, free of charge, the light of his word and his commandments to all who desire it.

Salvation

In Hebrew, the name "Jesus" means the Lord saves. Jesus is the Savior. He frees humanity from the grip of sin and evil. He lifts us from death and brings us to eternal life. He clears out our selfishness and gives us strength to become more generous in sharing with one another. He removes fear from our hearts and teaches us to trust God.

Need

What do people
need to live happily?

The Bible
tells us that faith in
Christ brings lasting peace.

He conquered
death by rising
from the tomb.

People need
the joy that comes
from life in Christ.

He is waiting
to freely give
his gift of life.

A life of peace
even in a world
cursed by sin
and death.

For Jesus also
promises to one day
bring lasting harmony.

In that day
all people will
acknowledge that
Jesus is the Christ.

This is the Jesus
that lives today!

CHAPTER 2

Free Them!

This mural presents Christ in his divine glory, holding a scroll in his hand. He wears the clothes worn by rulers of the artist's day: a heavy tunic covered by a long coat. Yellow, the principal color in this work, reinforces Christ's majesty and power.

Mural of the Basilica of the Saints Cosmas and Damien, representing the triumphant Christ, Rome (Italy)

© Frantisek Zvardon

The Return to Nazareth

Jesus as a Youth in the Carpenter Workshop of Joseph, stained glass of the Cathedral of Châlons-en-Champagne (France)

Jesus lives in Nazareth for thirty years. There he learns the trade of a carpenter. It's a place where everyone knows him. One day he decides to leave his village, which surprises his friends and family. "Why doesn't he stay with us?" they ask. "He has a house and a job in Nazareth. What gave him the idea to leave his home!"

Soon, the people of Nazareth hear about what Jesus is doing throughout the region. Some admire him, others criticize him, and still others want to get rid of him.

Luke and the First Christians

When Luke tells the story of the public life of Jesus, he places the visit of Jesus to Nazareth at the very beginning of his Gospel. Luke shows how Jesus outlined his plan for ministry and teaching in the local synagogue. In so doing, Jesus will follow the words spoken centuries before by the prophet Isaiah: Jesus will preach to the poor and to the prisoners, and he will bring freedom to those who suffer (Luke 4.16-19).

Nazareth Today (Galilee)

Throughout his Gospel, Luke focuses on what Jesus did for the poor, the sick, the prisoners, and the oppressed.* But Luke also thinks about

the unfortunate people of his own day. As a doctor, he meets many sick men and women. He travels extensively,** passing beggars on the roadside along the way. He sees slaves working in the ports and prisoners on boats and in jails. In writing these words, Luke lists people whom Jesus had in mind when he announced his plan of freedom there in the synagogue. But, like some people of Nazareth, not everyone welcomes Jesus' Good News.

The Prisoner

* The oppressed
The oppressed includes all those struck by illness, crushed by the cruelty of others, or suffering miserably because of poverty, unemployment, or loneliness.

** Travels extensively
Luke traveled with the apostle Paul on several trips throughout Asia and the Mediterranean world to preach the Good News of Jesus Christ.

The Mission of Jesus

Luke 4.16-24 (excerpts)

Jesus went back to Nazareth where he had been brought up, and as usual he went to the meeting place on the Sabbath. When he stood up to read from the Scriptures, he was given the book of Isaiah the prophet. He opened it and read,

"The Lord's Spirit
    has come to me
because he has chosen me
to tell the good news
    to the poor.
The Lord has sent me
to announce freedom for prisoners,
to give sight to the blind,
to free everyone
    who suffers,
and to say, 'This is the year
    the Lord has chosen.'"

Jesus closed the book, then handed it back to the man in charge and sat down. Everyone in the meeting place looked straight at Jesus.

Then Jesus said to them, "What you have just heard me read has come true today."

All the people started talking about Jesus and were amazed at the wonderful things he said. They kept asking, "Isn't he Joseph's son?"

Jesus answered, ... "You can be sure that no prophets are liked by the people of their own hometown."

Sabbath

All pious Jews went to the house of prayer (the synagogue) on the Sabbath (our Saturday). Like his fellow countrymen, Jesus faithfully practiced his religion.

Isaiah

Isaiah is the most important prophet of the Old Testament. He lived eight centuries before Jesus Christ. His words were saved in the sacred books of Israel.

Today

The words of Isaiah were written on sheepskin. Jesus prophesied that he himself was the fulfillment of Isaiah's prophecies.

New Times

Disturbance

As soon as men and women begin to take the Gospel seriously and put it into practice — whether in a family, a work group, a neighborhood, or a town — they run the risk

of disturbing people with their words and actions! Even those closest to them have trouble understanding what they're doing. They may say things like, "Who do you think you are preaching at us like that? Do you think you're better than everyone else? What right do you have to teach us how to live our lives?"

Good News

The Good News is that Jesus Christ came to free mankind from the penalty of sin! Through his sacrificial death on the cross, God's requirement that someone pay the penalty for sin was met. Jesus gave up his life for you and me, so that we could live forever with our Creator. Salvation is free for the asking.

Change

History shows that in every age many people live unhappy lives. There are always people who are poor, broken hearted, deprived of freedom, sick, unloved, and victims of hate and war crimes. To bring about a change in all this, Jesus' goal was to rid the world of whatever makes people slaves to evil, both within themselves and from without. Those who believe in Jesus continue this mission even today.

Christians

Those who believe the Good News of the Gospel and declare that Jesus is Lord, and that God raised him from the dead, are saved for all time (Romans 10:9). Through Jesus' Spirit, believers possess the power to do things that give hope to all people. They work to share the Good News with people everywhere who haven't had a chance to hear about Jesus. This is the task of all believers.

Deliverance

Words are promises.
Acts accomplish promises!

To accomplish the Good News,
to make it seen
everywhere and by everyone,
action is necessary –

Action that frees from pain
those who are trapped in sorrow;

Action that frees from unjust judgments
those who are prisoners of bad reputation;

Action that frees from hunger
 those who never have bread;

 Action that frees from war
those who must hide from bombs;

Action that frees from oppression
those who cannot go about at will;

Action that frees from poverty
those trapped in misery and want;

Action that frees from despair
those torn apart by daily suffering.

Who will perform these actions
of liberation for our brothers
and sisters
if not you and me?

CHAPTER • 3

Happiness!

**Joducus
or Josse II
the young
De Momper**
(1564-1635),
*The Sermon on
the Mount*

A majestic and magical mountain creates the background of this familiar scene. The characters and landscape are vivid with realistic details. The artist De Momper has placed this representation of the Sermon on the Mount in a setting from his own period, seventeenth century Flemish society.

© Bridgeman-Giraudon, Johnny van Haeften Gallery, London (England)

In the Times of Jesus

Pilgrims assembled on the Mount of Blessings (Galilee)

Jesus preaches his message to common, ordinary people. He meets and spends time with poor peasants ruined by taxation, sick people excluded from society, people mourning the death of a loved one, beggars, slaves, and widows without a means to live. These people probably can't imagine any change to their hopeless situation. In their misery, Jesus announces, "Things will change! You will be happy. In fact, you can be happy now!"

Toward the End of the First Century

Matthew the Evangelist gathered together many of the central teachings and acts of Jesus several years after his public ministry.* The Sermon on the Mount (chapters 5–7) includes such familiar words as the "Blessings" (or "Beatitudes") and Jesus' teachings about anger and love.

Matthew shares with Luke a concern for the poor. Four years of war between the Jews and the Romans (from A.D. 66 to 70) have resulted in the death of many people and have made slaves of many others. Cities and villages in the countryside are destroyed. More than ever it is important to share, to make peace, and to work for justice.

Also during this time the Christians are suffering persecution at the hands of Roman rulers.** They are hunted down, brought before judges, tortured, and executed because of their belief in Jesus and the Good News.

Jesus' words known as the "Blessings" (Matthew 5.2-12) were surely words of comfort to those who suffered from poverty and persecution in Matthew's day. Matthew wrote his Gospel for them – but not only for them.

Matthew on the Shoulders of the Prophet Isaiah, stained glass of the Chartes Cathedral (France)

Roman Soldier, Saint-Angel Bridge, Rome (Italy)

* Several years after his public ministry
The Gospel of Matthew was probably written between A.D. 80 and 90, almost sixty years after Jesus had preached in Judea.

** Persecution
The first major persecution of Christians was ordered by the Roman Emperor Nero. In A.D. 64, he falsely accused the Christians of having set Rome on fire.

15

The Blessings of Jesus

Matthew 5.1-10

When Jesus saw the crowds, he went up on the side of a mountain and sat down.

Jesus' disciples gathered around him, and he taught them:

"God blesses those people
who depend only on him.
They belong to the kingdom
of heaven!
God blesses those people
who grieve.
They will find comfort!
God blesses those people
who are humble.
The earth will belong
to them!
God blesses those people
who want to obey him
more than to eat or drink.
They will be given
what they want!
God blesses those people
who are merciful.
They will be treated
with mercy!
God blesses those people
whose hearts are pure.
They will see him!
They will be called
his children!
God blesses those people
who are treated badly
for doing right.
They belong to the kingdom
of heaven.

The Kingdom of Heaven

The contemporaries of Jesus awaited the arrival of the Kingdom of Heaven (or of God). Many hoped that God himself would come and restore justice, peace and joy for everyone. Jesus says, "The Kingdom is already here!"

Want To Obey Him More Than To Eat or Drink

God calls us to give up the things of the world, but then, in an amazing act of love, he promises to meet all our needs. The true disciple of Christ yearns to have the attitude of a servant and acts accordingly.

Now

Frantic Search

Every person in every age in every country desires happiness. All people dream of living in peace and joy without fearing things that will shatter their dreams and deepest desires.

Happiness

What is happiness? For some it's a small piece of bread, any kind of shelter from the rain, or a job where they put skills to use and earn a living. For others, happiness is financial independence, a place of authority and respect in society, or lots of things. For still others, it is an opportunity to love and be loved, a chance to give and receive, a way to bring peace and freedom to others, the right to believe in God, an occasion to bring equality for all.

Wretchedness

Human misery is everywhere – in countries left in poverty, in entire populations abandoned in hunger, in nations lacking knowledge of democracy and freedom, in entire regions being forced to surrender to war and terrorism. So many people are persecuted for their beliefs! So many tears have been shed because of exile and oppression! So much happiness is denied by selfishness and indifference!

The Call

Jesus teaches that God is deeply concerned about our happiness. Jesus calls and helps human beings to obtain a happiness that nothing can destroy – not even death. The Gospels repeat this good news over and over. Wouldn't it be absurd to kneel before God in adoration without doing our part to seek and obtain happiness for all God's children?

It Is for Today

Some people think
that the Beatitudes of the Mount
announce a future happiness
to come much later,
in heaven!

The mission of Jesus
is clear –
the happiness he speaks of
is to be built here on earth, now!

The mission of Jesus reverses
the human image of happiness.
It is not wealth
or strength, or domination
that provide beatitude.

It is in love of God
that happiness is rooted.
It is in sharing with the poor
and in the hope within grief.
It is in tenderness more powerful
than violence
and in the unlimited distribution of joy.
It is in forgiveness offered for trespasses
that happiness is found!

This happiness
reverses old habits
so common on earth.
This happiness is so big
that it needs God
to bring it to completion.

Share!

The *Very Rich Hours of the Duke of Berry* is one of the most beautiful Books of Hours of the Middle Ages. This work is a collection of prayers and liturgical elements chosen by the Duke of Berry. Each Book of Hours has a calendar illustrating the cycle of the seasons, agricultural works, and religious scenes. The vividly colored miniature presents Christ performing the multiplication of the loaves and fishes before the crowd. The presence of God adds a sense of solemn reverence to the scene.

Pol de Limbourg (fifteenth century),
Very Rich Hours of the Duke of Berry
Multiplication of Bread and Fish
(ms.65/1284 fol 168v)

© Giraudon, Museum of Condé, Chantilly (France)

Some Bread and Some Fish

Lake Tiberias (Galilee)

It is springtime. Even in Judea the grass is green. After many months of activity in Galilee, Jesus is well known. People come from everywhere to see him. It is impossible for him to get away from the crowds. They follow him and listen all day long.

As night falls, people must eat. How will this large crowd ever have enough to eat? There are two solutions – buy* enough bread for all or share what can found among them. A boy brings five loaves of bread and two fish.** But is this enough?

Jesus asks the crowd to stretch out on the green grass. He no doubt recites a traditional Jewish prayer, "Blessed are you, God our Lord, who has produced this bread for us." Then he shares the bread and fish with everyone by passing them around. There is plenty to go around with some left over! Everyone is satisfied.

Dried fish on a beach

The Memory of the Shared Bread

The first Christians never forgot this act of Jesus. In fact, the gospel writers repeat the story of the multiplication of the bread six different times! Why is that? Perhaps they wanted to stress these two truths:

1. The importance of sharing. Making a great deal of money to buy everything we want is not what is most important. People who buy and sell carry out business transactions. People who share show their love for one another. The first Christians are always reminded to share whatever they have with the poor.

Family meal

2. The importance of sharing the memory of Jesus' final supper with his disciples (Matthew 26.26-30). When the early Christians shared bread and wine they believed they were sharing the body and blood of Jesus himself. Sharing such a meal with the family of God is a way of becoming one with Christ himself.

* To buy
To buy enough bread for such a crowd would probably take two hundred silver coins. One coin is equivalent to a day's wage for an average worker.

** Bread and fish
This was a typical meal for the people who lived near the lake. The fish were grilled or dried.

The Sign of Sharing

John 6.1-14 (excerpts)

Jesus crossed Lake Galilee,… A large crowd had seen him work miracles to heal the sick, and those people went with him…. Jesus went up on a mountain with his disciples and sat down.

When Jesus saw the large crowd coming toward him, he asked Philip, "Where will we get enough food to feed all these people?…"

Philip answered, "Don't you know that it would take almost a year's wages just to buy only a little bread for each of these people?"

Andrew, the brother of Simon Peter, was one of the disciples. He spoke up and said, "There is a boy here who has five small loaves of barley bread and two fish. But what good is that with all these people?"

The ground was covered with grass, and Jesus told his disciples to have everyone sit down. About five thousand men were in the crowd. Jesus took the bread in his hands and gave thanks to God. Then he passed the bread to the people, and he did the same with the fish, until everyone had plenty to eat.

The people ate all they wanted, and Jesus told his disciples to gather up the leftovers so that nothing would be wasted….

After the people had seen Jesus work this miracle, they began saying, "This must be the Prophet who is to come into the world!"

Covered with Grass

In Israel, the grass grows in the spring and then dries out a few weeks afterward. According to the gospels, the sharing of the bread took place just before Passover.

Gave Thanks to God

In reporting the action of Jesus' Last Supper, all the Gospels use similar words, *"He broke the bread and handed it to his apostles. Then he said, 'This is my body, which is given for you'"* (Luke 22.19).

Miracle (Sign)

The Gospel of John speaks not so often of "miracles" but of "signs." A miracle is to be admired. One tries to understand the meaning of a sign.

Bread for Everyone

Hunger

Some people will never experience real hunger! Yet hunger is found in all countries, even in those we call "developed." It is a sad realization that some people have no other choice than to beg for the smallest amounts of food. They must depend on the kindness of others which is often hard to find. They have no other option than to plead with some hope for rescue.

Questions

How is it possible in a world where wealth always seems to increase and people suffer from overeating, that there are men, women, and children who die every day from hunger? Why are so many people forced to depend on the charity of others each and every day? Is it possible for a person to be happy while suffering the gnawing pains of unending hunger? How can we help so that everyone has enough bread to stay alive?

Bread

Overcoming physical hunger is indeed an important thing to do, but the Bible tells us the real answer to poverty and suffering. Scripture tells us that when people understand that Jesus is the Bread of Life, the entire body, including the spirit, is refreshed and nourished forever. Jesus also calls us to practical work, such as helping feed and clothe the poor.

To Multiply

All human beings have a right to bread. It is God's intention. So it is our duty to see that those around us have bread. Otherwise, happiness will be only a dream for the poor and oppressed among us. Every Christian who seriously wants to follow in the footsteps of Jesus will take very seriously the responsibility of sharing the loaves and fish, even when there are only a few.

The Strength of Sharing

Sharing is stronger than science,
stronger even than the power
of world leaders!

Sharing has the strength
to change the world!

Sharing has the strength
to open hearts trapped in their selfish
pleasures,
to make them welcoming
to calls of distress.

Sharing has the strength
to loosen clinging fingers
clasping their treasures
and fill them with offerings.

Sharing has the strength
to distribute to the hungry,
to quiet violence from lips
all too ready to spit out
hate and spite.
It breaks down walls
to allow those outside
to enter.

Sharing has the strength
to change the human heart
by drawing it above
selfish instinct
to noble heights
of self-forgetting compassion
and Christ-like
love of the neighbor.

Love!

Christ of the Saint-Leon Chapel at Eguisheim (France)

This mural presents a powerful and magnificent Jesus Christ. The lines of his face are soft and convey wisdom and dignity. The halo surrounding his head creates a circle of heavenly light. These are the ways the artist offers a portrait of a peaceful and benevolent Jesus Christ, both human and divine.

© Patrice Thébault

The Example of Jesus

Jesus Heals a Paralyzed Man, stained glass of the Cathedral of Châlons-en-Champagne (France)

Jesus went about Judea doing good. All those who met him along his way saw how much he loved them. He paid attention to the poor. He welcomed children.* He touched lepers.** He healed the sick. He forgave sins. He welcomed foreigners. His open and loving heart was evident to every person.

But he also became angry when someone was not treated fairly and given due respect.

For Jesus, the most important commandments in the Law of Moses are two: Love God with all your heart, soul, and mind; and love others as much as you love yourself.

Jesus on the Cross, Sélestat (France)

Afterward-better Understanding

Each of the Gospels keep alive the memory of Jesus' love and his teaching that love is the most important commandment. After his death and resurrection, the Gospel writers saw more clearly why the leaders of the people*** had condemned and crucified Jesus. They remembered the tremendous love he showed for all people in the words he spoke on the cross, "Father, forgive them." The first Christians also came to understand better and better the saying of Jesus, *"The greatest way to show love for friends is to die for them."* That is what Jesus did.

John writes his Gospel toward the end of the first century A.D. He clearly shows that Jesus summarizes his entire ministry in the command to love.

* The children
Even Jesus' disciples tried to keep children away from Jesus, thinking they would disturb him while he taught others.

** The lepers
The Law of Moses forbid anyone to approach or touch a leper for fear of spreading the disease.

*** The leaders of the people
The high priests of the Temple and the Roman governor, Pontius Pilate, were afraid that Jesus would head a rebellion that might anger Rome.

The Most Important Commandment

John 15.12-17

Now I tell you to love each other, as I have loved you. The greatest way to show love for friends is to die for them. And you are my friends, if you obey me. Servants don't know what their master is doing, and so I don't speak to you as my servants. I speak to you as my friends, and I have told you everything that my Father has told me.

You did not choose me. I chose you and sent you out to produce fruit, the kind of fruit that will last. Then my Father will give you whatever you ask for in my name. So I command you to love each other.

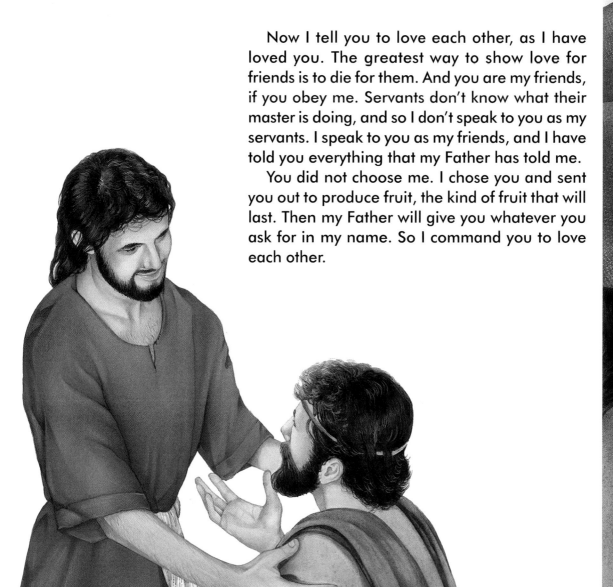

I Tell You

The commandment of love replaces and synthesizes the hundreds of prescriptions of the Jewish Law.

As

Jesus' commandment of love requires more than merely the love we give to those who love us. It asks us to love as Jesus loved, that is to love even our enemies, and to be willing to give up our lives for others.

Servants

In the languages of the Bible (Hebrew and Greek), one word is used to mean both a slave and a servant.

Love Is the Most Important

The Law of Love

Laws are necessary. They are required by a society to safeguard people's rights. They primarily have one goal – to allow people to live together in peace with mutual respect. Jesus did not write any new laws or commandments. For him, there was only one law – the law of love! This law is the foundation of every other law.

Love!

Love can be expressed in many different ways. The love that Jesus speaks about is not just a feeling in one's heart. It shows itself in outward actions. It expresses itself in practical words and deeds. To love is to bring happiness to another, to forgive, to console those in pain, to share with the poor, to give bread to the hungry, to stand by the sick. How else is love shared?

Friends of Jesus

Those who believe in Jesus are not slaves under his control like people in a cult! It is not fear that drives us to follow Jesus. It is love. Our love for Jesus makes us happy and free to love others. Our desire should be to help others know about the love of Jesus by showing them love.

Sign

We do not distinguish ourselves as Christians by our clothes, our praying, our shunning of evil, or our pity of others. The true sign that we are Jesus' disciples is our love of others, especially those who are hurting and who suffer from unhappiness. It is not wearing a cross that makes a Christian but rather the love we have for others… even our enemies!

A World of Love

Jesus came to create
a world of love.
Those who consider themselves
his friends,
feel irresistibly drawn to assist him
to accomplish this goal.

The world of love
becomes reality
when people are no longer judged
by their appearances,
when people are no longer put into categories –
those to avoid and
those to associate with –
when understanding rules
in spite of opposing ideas,
when mutual respect is established
in spite of different nationalities,
when neighbors are no longer considered
competitors,
but brothers and sisters –
people just like us
to share with –
when power
is used to help the weak,
when wealth
is shared with the poor,
when people offer
their knowledge and wisdom
to those trapped
in ignorance.

In the construction lot
of the world of love still
being built,
many workers
are awaited.

Witnesses

Throughout the centuries, thousands of men and women have lived out the ministry of Jesus. Some have remained hidden and unknown. Others are famous and remembered long after they lived. Read one example of such a witness for Jesus.

Sir Vincent

Saint Vincent de Paul was born in a small village in the Landes of France in 1580. His parents

were poor peasants. Vincent began helping them by guarding pigs. The priest noticed the child's quick mind and had him sent to school. In time Vincent became a priest and hoped to find a good position at the court of the King of Paris.

But meeting the poor changed Vincent's life. There were so many people in need. In Paris alone there were some forty thousand beggars. Vincent asked for the help of men and women around him to rescue the poor, to save the abandoned children, and to care for the hospitalized, the sick, or those wounded in war. Sir Vincent, as he was called, died in 1660. He never became a bishop or a monsignor, but he dedicated his life to helping the poor. His life can be summarized in the motto, "The poor are our masters."

Saint Vincent de Paul (eighteenth century), © Lauros-Giraudon, Castle of Versailles, Versailles (France)

Martin Luther King

Martin Luther King was an African American pastor in the United States. During his lifetime, African Americans and whites did not share the same rights. Violent riots broke out in some cities. There were bombings and killings. Martin Luther King wanted to defend his African American brothers, but not with violence. He dreamed of the day "when the sons of old slaves and those of new masters will sit at the table of fraternity."

Despite persistent opposition, he continued his action for justice. He organized non-violent marches of poor people, boycotts of buses reserved for African Americans, and sit-ins in empty buildings.

He was often wanted by the police and attacked by members of violent groups of his own people. But in 1964, he received the Noble Peace Prize. The evening of April 3, 1968, he spoke at a demonstration. A shot was fired. Martin Luther King was struck down and died one hour later. He had once said, "I tried to spend my life putting clothes on the naked, feeding the hungry, and loving and serving humanity."

Sophie Scholl

In the early 1940s, Hitler ruled as a dictator in Nazi Germany. Everyone had to submit to his rule. Those who refused were thrown into prison or tortured. He was determined to destroy the Jewish people by killing every Jew alive. Hitler wanted to take over all of Europe. It soon became a war zone. Few people dared to speak out against him publicly. Certain Christians, though, tried to resist.

In 1942 Sophie Scholl, a student in Munich, was twenty-one years old. With her brother Hans and some friends, she founded the "White Rose." This movement issued pamphlets to make people reflect on the absurdity of the dictatorship and the war.

Soon the members of the White Rose were arrested by the secret police. On February 22, 1942, Sophie, her brother and a friend were tried and condemned. Half an hour later, they are beheaded by ax in a prison courtyard. They are dead, but their example lives on.

Rigoberta Menchû

In 1959 Rigoberta was born to a native family in Guatemala. She was the sixth of nine children. From the age of nine she had to work harvesting coffee. She watched her brother and a best friend die from the poison of insecticides sprayed by planes onto the coffee fields. When her investigation led her to see the injustice done to the poor natives working the mega-plantations, she began a revolution.

Her father was threatened with imprisonment, kidnapped, tortured and left half dead. Soldiers harassed the village. Under her leadership, the people organized to defend themselves. Rigoberta explained her action in this way, "For me, one thing is important, the life of Christ… He went so far as to sacrifice his life. But Christ's life is not over. Each generation continues it."

In 1992 Rigoberta received the Nobel Peace Prize. Today, she continues her efforts to bring people together for the cause of justice to the native population of Guatemala.

You certainly have learned about or know other heroes and witnesses to the love of Jesus. What do you do to show love to others?

Titles already published:

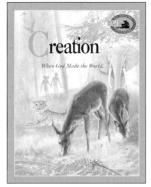
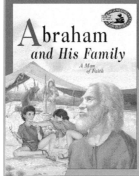
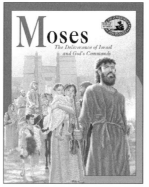
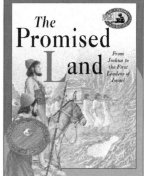

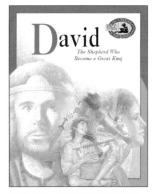
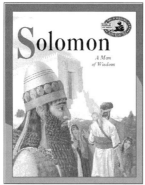
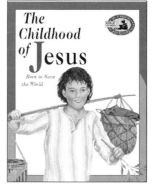
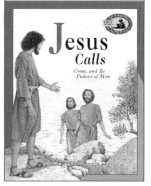

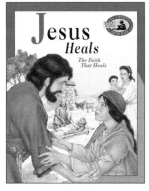
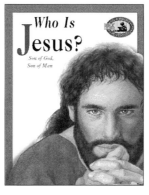
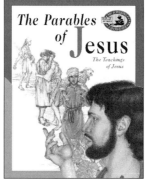

Forthcoming titles in the JUNIOR BIBLE Collection:

- The First Prophets
- Passion and Resurrection
- Exile and Return
- Isaiah, Micah, Jeremiah
- Jesus and the Outcasts
- Jesus in Jerusalem
- Acts
- Wisdom
- Psalms
- Women
- Revelation
- Letters

The Country of Jesus

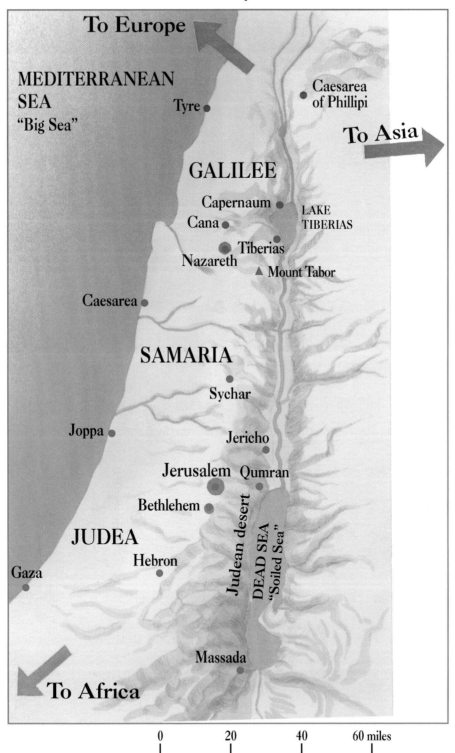

The Mission of Jesus

ORIGINAL TEXT BY

Meredith HARTMAN, Karim BERRADA,

Loretta PASTVA, SND,

Albert HARI, Charles SINGER

ENGLISH TEXT ADAPTED BY

the American Bible Society

PHOTOGRAPHY

Frantisek ZVARDON, Alsace Média,

René MATTÈS, Patrice THÉBAULT

ILLUSTRATORS

Mariano VALSESIA, Betti FERRERO

MIA. Milan Illustrations Agency

LAYOUT

Bayle Graphic Studio

FIRST PRINTING: NOVEMBER 2000

For information write: Master Books, P.O. Box 727, Green Forest, AR 72638.

ISBN: 0-89051-326-0

Master Books

ÉDITIONS
DU SIGNE
© ÉDITIONS DU SIGNE 1997